How to Make Money at Home

Entrepreneur Book Series

M. Usman

Mendon Cottage Books

JD-Biz Publishing

Download Free Books!

http://MendonCottageBooks.com

All Rights Reserved.

No part of this publication may be reproduced in any form or by any means, including scanning, photocopying, or otherwise without prior written permission from JD-Biz Corp Copyright © 2015

All Images Licensed by Fotolia and 123RF.

Check out our other Entrepreneur books

Download Free Books!
http://MendonCottageBooks.com

Table of Contents

Preface..4
Chapter # 1: An Introduction to Making Money....................................5
Chapter # 2: Affiliate Marketing..8
Chapter # 3: Freelancing..11
Chapter # 4: Get Paid to Search...14
Chapter # 5: Get Paid to Watch Videos...16
Chapter # 6: Publish Books...18
Chapter # 7: Rent Your Car...21
Chapter # 8: Rent Your Home...23
Chapter # 9: Start an Online Store...26
Chapter # 10: Teach Your Skills..29
Conclusion...31
References...32
Author Bio...33
Publisher..44

Preface

Have you always wanted to make enough money to support yourself without stepping a foot in an office? If yes, this book will show you everything you need to know about how to start making money working from home.

This trend has become very popular in recent years, because of the internet. Unfortunately, it has also led to a rise in scammers who charge lots of money only to give you information that does not make you any money in the end.

There are a lot of ways you can make money while at home. Some of these will make you rich, while others will only make you enough to buy a cup of coffee.

In this book, there is no hype. I will show you what works and what doesn't. If you have been looking for legitimate ways to make money while at home, this is a book you must read.

Chapter # 1: An Introduction to Making Money

There is no such thing as easy money; if you want to be rich, you must work hard. You should stop searching for an easy way to prosper, because the truth is that it does not exist. You will waste your time jumping from one thing to another. In the end, you will throw in the towel, convinced that making money is impossible for you.

However, you can make a lot of money and in a lot of ways. Here are the steps you must follow.

Find a Niche

A niche refers to a specific area of work that you are an expert in. For example, it could be that you love music and have a lot knowledge about it, so DJing is a niche you can follow. Or you may start aquaculture if you are really into fish.

As you can see, there is no limit to how many ways you can use to make money.

However, it is important to ensure that the niche you choose is profitable. You do not want to get into something and discover that it is not lucrative, when you are already knee-deep in it.

So how do you find out?

You can ask people who have worked in the niche. Additionally, a search on the internet will also give you almost everything you may need to know.

Mistakenly, many believe that profitability is the only thing they can use to decide if they should start making money using a certain niche. They forget that money can, sometimes, cease to be a motivator. So, when making your selection, choose something that you love. You will not start making money instantly with it, but your love for it is what will keep you going.

Hard Work Pays

Whatever way you choose to make money with, will require hard work. You have made your choice, now there is no rest for the weary. You will need to put in hours of learning and practice to become the best.

You will experience heartaches and headaches along the way, but that is what leads to success. You must endure whatever obstacle you will meet in your niche.

The difference between successful people and failures is that those who are successful rise when they fall and keep on moving. But failures jump to another ship.

Don't be fooled by "get rich quickly" programs as a way of making money, because they do not work. The people selling these are rich because you pay them to access their so-called brilliant ways to get rich.

You do not need to waste money when trying to make money. There is a lot of free stuff these days that you can use to learn how to prosper.

Lastly, understand that it will take time to start making money if you are new in any niche. There is no such thing as overnight success, because years of hard work and practice are usually hidden behind the curtain.

Now that we have made a few things clear, let's go on to look at the ways you can use to make money at home.

Chapter # 2: Affiliate Marketing

Affiliate marketing is probably one of the most difficult ways you can use to make money. But once you get good at it, it is very lucrative. In fact, it is the last job you will ever want.

What Is Affiliate Marketing

Affiliate marketing refers to the process of advertising someone's product to potential customers. In return to your effort, you get a percentage of the money made in the sale. Specifically, this starts from 1% to 10%. But it is not surprising to find it as high as 70% when dealing with software products.

If you have the guts, you can start affiliate marketing today. There are no special qualifications or certificates you need to possess. Sweetening the deal even further, you have the freedom to choose which products you are going to market.

How to Get Started

The product you are trying to market will dictate the best route you will need to take to make the sale. In this chapter, we will assume that the product can be sold online and so, you will be marketing it on the web.

1. Choose the Product You Want to Market

The first step is to choose a product that you will be advertising. If you miss this important step, you will have no idea of what the website will be about. You can market weight loss products, softwares, clothes, juicers, golf equipment, etc.

2. Create a Website

Now, you can make a website that is focused on what you are trying to sell. For example, if you want to market hunting gear, you can start a website that teaches people how to hunt. Or you may concentrate on reviewing hunting gear.

The internet is no longer the way it was decades ago. You can now have a website running in just minutes. And if you do not have any money, you can even create one for free. However, if you want to make a professional impression and win the trust of your customers, I advise that you buy a domain name and pay for hosting.

3. Create Content

No matter how good looking your website is, let alone how fancy its name is, it will not go far if it does not have content. Pasting affiliate links everywhere will scare away both customers and search engines.

On the other hand, great content will enable your website to rank highly in search results. So you will get a lot of visitors to your website.

At the same time, content that helps people will win you their trust. They will be reaching for their wallets to buy every product that you recommend.

4. Sign Up at Websites to be an Affiliate Marketer

Almost all websites that sell products online have an affiliate program. If you know any that you would like to be associated with, head over to its website, and see if you can sign up as an affiliate.

Some popular websites with affiliate programs include, Amazon, EBay, ShareASale, Market Health, CJ (was known as Commission Junction), ClickBank, and other websites.

Once you have the affiliate links on your website, you will need to keep working hard if you want to see any money. There are a lot of websites on the internet which increases the competition you must overcome to get to the top.

With enough effort, you will see that you have started making more money with affiliate marketing. If others are making thousands every month doing the same thing, why would you fail?

The good news is that although a lot of people sign up for affiliate programs, just a few stay active.

Chapter # 3: Freelancing

Everyone is a master at something. So the only thing keeping you from making money with your skill is your inability to sell it to people who need it.

And if you have what it takes, you can sell that skill to a number of people, simultaneously, resulting in more money in your pocket.

What Is a Freelancer?

A freelancer is someone who is not permanently employed with any organization and works for whoever shows up with a job.

This means that the person offering work does not have any authority over the freelancer, except to ensure that work is delivered on time and is of an acceptable quality. In other words, a freelancer is his own boss.

He is the one who comes up with working hours, markets his skills to clients, takes the role of an accountant, etc. Freelancing is simply a one-man business.

There is no limit to how much you can make, as you can take as many projects as you can handle and charge as much as you think you deserve.

Freelancing includes job like writing, programming, marketing, human resource management, accounting, and more.

Pros of Freelancing

You Choose When and Where to Work from - You will not get stuck in traffic like other people who have to travel to the office. And if you feel like sleeping all day and working at night, you have the freedom to do just that.

Freedom to Raise Your Rate - If you think you deserve more for you skills, there is nothing stopping you from raising your rate. And this is what most freelancers do when they have gained some experience.

Cons of Freelancing

You Only Make Money When You Show Up - Unlike people who have a day job, you only make money when you are working. So if you break your neck and can't work for the next two weeks, it will be your loss.

Too Much Freedom - For other people, not having someone to supervise them can be problematic. Freelancing requires that you force yourself to work even when you do not want to.

Where to Start

If you have the guts to do it, you can earn a nice living as a freelancer. For example, those who have lots of experience make more than $60,000 a year.

But as a newbie, you will not be making that much. The trick is to work hard and learn everything you can about freelancing. With time, your skills will grow and so will your reputation. Getting work that pays well will not be a problem.

To get started as a freelancer, you need to identify skills you are good at. For example, you may be a proficient accountant, programmer, writer, etc. Once you have identified your skill, search for websites that have the type of work that you are looking for.

For a start, you can try PeoplePerHour, Freelancer, Upwork, and many other websites. If you also know local organizations that might use your skill, do not be afraid to approach them.

Chapter # 4: Get Paid to Search

We spend most of our time on the internet searching for things to buy, for entertainment purposes, and searching for other information. And without a doubt, most of these searches are done in Google. But did you know that you could get paid for searching online? This means you will make money, doing things you already do. No extra effort required!

If you have been looking for an easy way to make some money, this is your answer.

The thing is that Google has taken over the internet. In fact, I would not blame you if you said you do not know any other search engine. Making the problem even worse, most web browsers come with Google as the default search engine leaving the user with no option but use it.

As a survival strategy, other search engines are willing to lose money just to get their name in your browser. So they pay you for each search you make using their search engine. Unfortunately, Google is not among them.

However, one thing must be made clear before we go any further—you will not get rich doing this. I already said in the first chapter that making a substantial amount of money at home demands hard work. And clearly, searching online cannot, in any way, be described as hard work.

Before you sign up for an account at any of the websites below, I recommend that you take time to see their requirements. Additionally, you can also read some reviews by people who have been using these websites in the last couple of months to get a feel of what you should expect.

Here are the websites:

1. Swagbucks – This has been around for a long time and its reputation continues to grow every day. Unlike other money making websites, Swagbucks always pays. Once you reach the minimum payout, you can be guaranteed that you will buy yourself a cup of coffee.

2. Bing Rewards – Bing is a trusted website. In fact, it is the one search engine I would recommend after Google. Sweetening the deal is that you can register for Bing Rewards. So every time you make a search in Bing, you get points that you can redeem.

Other websites that will pay you for searching include Zoombucks, FusionCash, CashCrate, and Inbox Dollars.

With some of these sites, you will also get a chance to take part in online surveys. But again, you will not buy yourself a house taking these surveys.

Chapter # 5: Get Paid to Watch Videos

Humans love watching videos. Therefore, it is no wonder that websites like Youtube have become very popular. What you may not know, however, is that you can make money sitting in front of your computer watching videos.

Have you ever wondered why you go channel surfing when watching TV?

The reason is that there are a lot of advertisements on TV which do nothing but waste your time. But what you must remember is that all those ads were paid for by companies to have them in front of you.

So what if those companies could use that money to pay you to sit in front of your computer and watch their ads? And that is exactly how you make money by watching videos online.

However, the fact that these companies are paying a lot of money does not mean you will get rich overnight. Remember that you are not the only one who is watching these; other people all over the world are also online to share the same dollar that you are trying to make.

Adding to that, some adverts will not be available in your area.

Here are some of the websites that will pay you just to watch videos.

1. Paid2Youtube – The name says it all; you will get money for watching videos on Youtube. The payment is just 0.005 per video.

2. QuickRewards – Despite the name, you will not make rewards quickly at this website. But once you fulfill your tasks and reach the minimum payout, you get paid. Unfortunately, this website is only for people living in Canada, UK, and USA.

3. Swagbucks – This website also lets you watch videos and make money in the process.

4. InboxDollars – You will also find some videos here that will make you some money.

Chapter # 6: Publish Books

If you know you are good at writing, then you can start writing books as a way to make money. You just need to have a couple of them under your name and you can be guaranteed that dollars will be flooding in your account—even when you are asleep.

You can write about any topic that you want. If you fancy specializing in fiction, you have the liberty to do so. If non-fiction is your thing, then go for it.

However, like with all things, you will not make a lot of money with your first book. But that first book is what you need to get over the wall that defines writers from wannabes. As a matter of fact, most successful writers are ashamed with their first books.

How to Write a Book

Writing a book is not that hard. As long as you know how to put some words together to get your point across, you are good to go. But in order to become successful, you must learn from other writers and practice whatever they teach you.

Here is how you write a book:

1. Decide What You Want to Write About – Describe what it is you want the reader to get by the time he finishes reading your book. Be able to explain this in just one sentence. Do you want to tell him how he can prevent Hepatitis C? Or would you like to teach him how to fix his car?

2. Make an Outline – This is something that details how your book will progress. If you skip this step, you will surely hit a block along the way. Even worse, your book will be all over the place and leave the reader confused and not knowing what you are trying to say.

3. Research – Depending on what you are writing about, you may need to do some research. Remember to stay focused on your theme or outline. Otherwise, you will waste time reading things you will not even use in the book.

4. Write – Writing should be easy and fun. You should not waste your energy trying to make the book perfect at this stage, or you will not write. Go with whatever comes to mind as long as you are following your outline and information you gathered in the research stage. This is no time to be making corrections. If you misspelled a certain word, keep going. If you think the last sentence does not sound right, pretend you have no "Backspace" key. Just focus on getting to the end.

5. Edit – Once you are done writing, this is the stage where you have all the freedom to make any corrections. You will see that some sentences may need deleting, new sections may have to be inserted, grammar fixed, and more. You will also discover that the book may sound better when you rearrange some sections.

Editing takes time. You may have to do it 3 or 4 times to get the book to sound the way you want.

6. Get Someone to Review Your Book – No matter how good you are, you will need a new set of eyes to review your book; this means getting other people to read it. For better results, be ready to spend money on hiring an expert. Relatives and friends are not the best option.

7. Design Book – If you know nothing about designing, it is recommended that you hire someone who does. A lot of people judge a book by its cover despite knowing that they shouldn't do so. So do yourself, and the book, a favor and get a professional designer.

8. Publish Your Book – There are a number of websites that will let you publish your book. One of them is Amazon.

9. Advertise – Since this chapter assumes that you will publish the book yourself, know that you are responsible for advertising. You may use guest blogging, social media, or any other ways you can imagine.

Chapter # 7: Rent Your Car

You probably do not use your car that much. If you are not using it to go shopping, then you are probably using it to take you to work. However, considering that the cost of running a car keeps on rising, it's a good idea to make it pay for some of its expenses. So whenever it is free, you can rent it.

Depending on where you live and the availability of renters, you can earn a living just by letting people use your car. You can charge $10 per hour or $40-70 per day. So, on average, expect to have $1000 per month of extra income in your pocket.

If you are like a lot of people, however, the idea of renting your car to strangers should surely send chills running down your spine. You may ask yourself, What if it gets involved in an accident? What if the renter runs away with it?

Fortunately for you, those kinds of situations are not common. But you cannot expect to run away from little nuisances like the smell of smoke in your car, a can of beer in the back seat, etc.

To ensure that someone is responsible in case the unthinkable happens to your car, you must sign up with a rental company. At the moment, you can register at RelayRides or GetAround.

In order to be accepted, you must have a car that is not older than 10 years, and additionally, it must be in a great condition.

Once you have registered for an account at those websites and have been given an account, you will not need to do a lot of work on your part. Sit at home, watch TV, eat, and exercise. Your car will be working for you. And if you find that you are making a substantial amount of money with one car, you have all the reasons to invest in another one.

Chapter # 8: Rent Your Home

If you have spare rooms in your house, then you have an opportunity to earn money easily. You can rent them to people who are in need of shelter.

Depending on where you live and how many rooms you have, this is a very sustainable way of making money. Think about it, your house is yours for as long as you want. And since not everyone can have a house of his own, you can bet that you will never run out of customers.

However, the biggest setback that comes with renting your home is repairs, and these can get expensive. You will need to fix broken pipes, paint the house, install new windows, and more.

Furthermore, you must have great negotiation skills

The most dangerous thing, however, is that you will be letting strangers come into your house. This puts both you and your family at risk, as you will not have much background information regarding your tenants. You may get robbed or even be attacked.

To avoid all that, it is important that everyone is screened before being given access into your house. If you know you cannot handle such work, then it is important that you hire a property manager to do everything on your behalf.

And before you get into the business of renting your home, it pays to be knowledgeable of the legal requirements that you must fulfill.

Ways of Making Money with Your House

Here they are:

1. Rent a Room – By following this method, you will let someone stay in a spare room in your house. However, this usually means he will be living in your home for a couple of months.

2. Turn a Room into a Boutique Hotel – This involves renting a room in your home for a night or just a few days. So, if you are against the idea of letting strangers live in your house for months, this is the way to go. Additionally, you will make more money if you can manage to get a lot of visitors every month. The most important thing is your location; it has to be accessible.

3. Let Your Home Be a Set – If you can find someone to use your home as a movie set, this is definitely something you must consider doing. Not only does it pay well, but it also usually only takes a couple of days. You can earn an average of $1000 per day. However, you will be required to evacuate the house whenever it is being used as a set.

In order to succeed in all three cases, you must advertise that your home is available for renting. At the same time, simply because it is your house, doesn't mean you can do whatever you want. Once you have received money from any of your tenants, even if he is just renting a room, give him the privacy he needs.

Chapter # 9: Start an Online Store

If you can anticipate what someone will want to buy, and deliver that thing better than anyone else, you can bet that you will have a successful business. Selling goods to other people is one of the most common ways of making money.

To get started, you just need to open an online store.

As the name suggests, you will be selling your products on the internet. There is no need to pay rent which will save you some money. At the same time, you have access to more customers because your store stays open all the time and anyone from anywhere can visit it.

However, being an online store means you will compete with other websites also selling products on the web.

On top of that, if you do not have skills in web designing, you may need to hire someone who does to assist you. So be prepared to spend money, as these services do not come cheap.

And if you thought it couldn't get any worse, you may also need to hire an SEO specialist to help optimize your website for higher rankings in search results. However, if you want to save money, there are platforms that will get your store running without the need for a web designer or an SEO specialist. Just know that these platforms lack options you may need to make your store the way you want.

How to Open an Online Store

1. Decide on What Products You Will Be Selling - The first step in this process is to decide what merchandise you will be selling. Although you can have everything in your store, it helps to pick a single product and focus all your effort on it.

Additionally, you will have the opportunity to know if the product will sell online (some things only do well when sold in person).

2. Make a Business Plan – Just like with a store in the bricks and mortar world, your online store also needs a business plan. This will give you a chance to determine if you have any chance of succeeding.

Actually, the lack of a business plan is one of the leading reasons most businesses cease to exist. If you know you are not good at making plans, it is recommended that you work with someone who understands the process.

3. Build a Website – Once you are convinced that you have a perfect business idea after working out your plan, you can register a domain name and pick a host for you website.

You will also need to fill out some legal documents because you are starting a business (this will differ depending on where you live).

Building a website is no walk in the park. It will take time and a lot of effort. If you are impatient to learn how to do it, you might as well hire someone to do it for you. Just ensure that you have enough money before you even get started.

And once the website is online, promote it through social media, forums, other websites, etc.

Chapter # 10: Teach Your Skills

As stated earlier in the book, everyone is good at something. You may be the most proficient guitarist in your area. Or you may be a great songwriter. Actually, the possibilities are endless. But what you may not realize is that someone is looking for you to teach him that skill.

If only you can find the person who needs your skills, your task will be reduced to convincing them that you have what they want, and they will get it for a certain fee. So, at the end of the day, you get money in your pocket.

There is no limit to what you can teach. For example, you can teach people how to make money, how to build a website, how to use social media for businesses, how to get your ex back, how to cook, play golf, paint a house, etc.

Do not be fooled into thinking that every topic has already been taught. You can breathe in some fresh air by presenting it from a new angle. Besides, some may want a one on one class.

Once you are established and have gained some experience, you can earn a nice living just by teaching. If you are just starting out, expect to earn $20 per hour. But as time goes, you will be able to charge higher rates as more people will begin to recognize you as an expert.

Also, depending on what it is you want to teach, you may need to have a college degree.

Where to Teach

There are a lot of places where you can find teaching opportunities.

Online – A number of websites on the internet will give you a chance to find teaching jobs. Making it even better, since you will be doing it on the web, you will likely meet a lot of people who need your services. Furthermore, you will not have a hard time find someone who needs the skill that you have, like if you are doing it locally.

Where You Live – You will probably find some local facilities that will give you an opportunity to teach your skill. If you cannot find any such facilities, you may put adverts in the local newspaper or on the internet.

However, know that it will not be easy to get started. People will first want to see proof that you are a competent teacher. But once you get a couple of teaching sessions, what follows will be easy.

Conclusion

I am sure this book has helped you discover some ways you can use to make money at home. Since you cannot do everything outlined in the book, I would recommend that you pick one method of making money and stick with it. Learn everything you can about it and strive to be the best. Understand that to get to the top, you will need to work very hard.

You must also remember that some of the methods in the book will not start making you money right off the bat. So be patient and keep yourself motivated.

If you always thought that making money while at home was impossible, this book has certainly proven you wrong. The best part is that you do not need any special qualifications to get started.

A lot of people are earning a living using the methods in this book, and you can do the same.

References

Image Links

https://pixabay.com/en/home-money-euro-coin-coins-167734/

https://pixabay.com/en/keyboard-apple-input-keys-hardware-338513/

https://pixabay.com/en/blogging-blogger-office-business-336375/

https://pixabay.com/en/blogging-computer-female-girl-15968/

https://pixabay.com/en/google-www-online-search-search-485613/

https://pixabay.com/en/apple-mac-computer-desktop-monitor-691282/

https://pixabay.com/en/writing-writer-notes-pen-notebook-923882/

https://pixabay.com/en/car-audi-headlight-red-light-368636/

https://pixabay.com/en/bed-pillows-bedroom-headboard-890579/

https://pixabay.com/en/money-card-business-credit-card-256319/

https://pixabay.com/en/board-training-coach-learn-784363/

Author Bio

Muhammad Usman is a distinguished medical graduate of Allama Iqbal medical college (AIMC). He is a professional writer who has been in the field for more than 4 years. During this time he has produced 10,000+ articles, blogs, and eBooks on various niches related to diseases, health, fitness, nutrition, and well-being. He is a regular contributor to several journals related to medicine and surgery. He is the editor of several journals and newspapers.

Check out some of the other JD-Biz Publishing books

[Gardening Series on Amazon](#)

Health Learning Series

[Country Life Books](#)

Health Learning Series

[Amazing Animal Book Series](#)

Learn To Draw Series

How to Build and Plan Books

Entrepreneur Book Series

Our books are available at

1. Amazon.com
2. Barnes and Noble
3. Itunes
4. Kobo
5. Smashwords
6. Google Play Books

Download Free Books!

http://MendonCottageBooks.com

Publisher

JD-Biz Corp
P O Box 374
Mendon, Utah 84325
http://www.jd-biz.com/

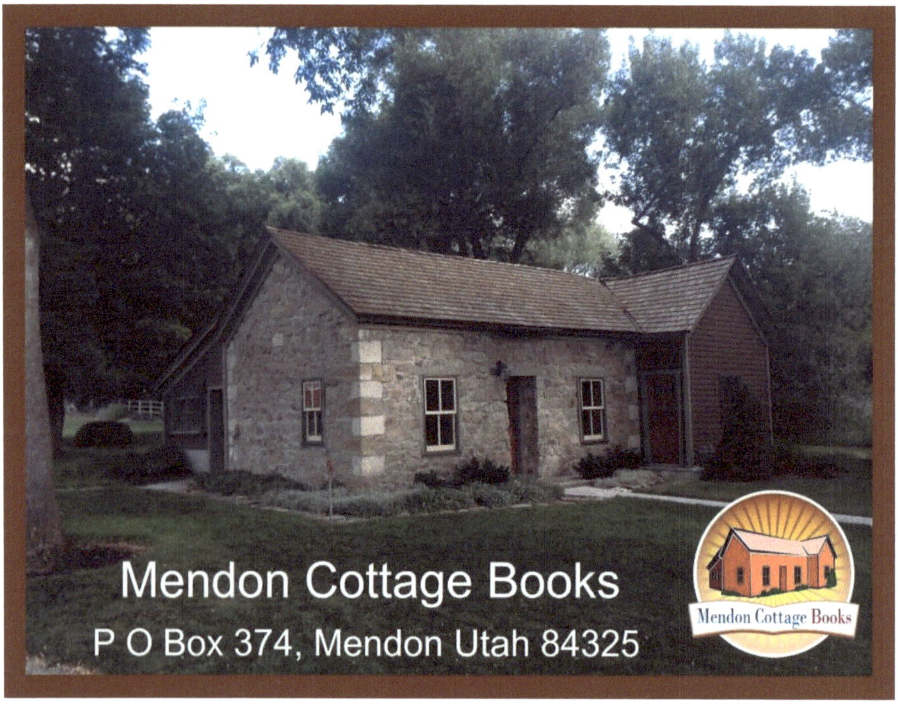

www.ingramcontent.com/pod-product-compliance
Lightning Source LLC
Chambersburg PA
CBHW040813200526

45159CB00022B/639